DEBT PAYOFF PLAN

Melford Alston

Copyright © 2010 by **Melford Alston**

All rights reserved. No part of this publication may be reproduced, stored in a retrieval system, or transmitted, in any form or by any means - electronic, mechanical, photocopying, recording, or any other - without prior written permission of the author and publisher.

Printed in the United States of America

First Printing September 2010

DISCLAIMER:

To the best of my ability and in my opinion all ideas, suggestions, techniques, and conclusions in this manual abide by local, state, and federal laws. The author and publisher, are not lawyers or tax advisors.

The reader is thus urged to consult legal counsel regarding any points of law and taxation.

The author and publisher make no guaranty or warranty as to the information provided herein will produce any particular results, and that the advice and strategies contained herein may not be suitable for every individual. Neither the author, nor publisher shall be liable for any loss of income or profit or any other damages – special, incidental or consequential.

TABLE OF CONTENTS

STEP ONE – Make a list of your bills 4
STEP TWO – Where to find the money to pay off your bills 5
STEP THREE – The process of paying off your bills....................12
SOMETHING TO THINK ABOUT 15

DEBT PAYOFF PLAN ©

By Melford Alston

Struggling just to make ends meet? Living paycheck to paycheck? Drowning in an ocean of debt? Too much month left at the end of the money? What you need is a plan to get out of debt. My 'Debt Payoff Plan' will do just that - get you out of debt.

No, this not about filing bankruptcy, or debt consolidation or debt settlement or debt counseling or debt negotiation. No, you do not have to take a debt management class along with this manual. And no, we are not a debt management company. But, we do have what you need to get out of debt fast …. and save money, too.

This plan is designed to completely pay off your bills/debts within months, including your large bills (car, house) which can be paid off years sooner. This is a very simple plan. It is such a simple debt payoff plan that at first look you might not believe that it will work and work quickly. **Try it! You have nothing to lose but debt, stress, and worry.** Your gain will be good credit, and more money to save, invest, and spend.

There are two roadways you can take to do this; the long way and the short way. The long way is to pay off 'first' the bills that have the highest interest rates and fees. Usually your largest or highest bills have the highest interest rates and fees. Some people will think that this is the proper way or the correct way to pay off their debt. That's ok …for them, but not for you. You need quick relief from the stress and worry.

I will NOT show you the long way. Why? Because most people will not continue through to the end to become debt free. Why? It's because of their mindset. Let's be real here. Most people have the instant gratification mindset: I want it NOW….give it to me NOW…. I am NOT going to continue to wait for it. Some even want it NOW even though they have not put forth any **effort** to receive it. I think you get my point. If most people had to work at paying off their debt for one year, **before** they could see <u>just</u> the first bill paid off, they would quit. I probably would too.

The big psychological benefits of comfort and confidence that you will get from quickly paying off one or two bills will greatly out weigh the difference in interest charges.

Important:

Once you start paying off your debt, your credit score will go up. When your credit gets better, and it will, please do NOT open any new credit card accounts. Why get out of debt if you are just going to go right back in debt? Once a credit card is paid off, don't close it. Leave the account open so that you will have credit that you are NOT using because this will help improve your credit score. Call the credit card companies that you have paid off and ask them to waive your annual fees on the cards. Do this because now you will be one of their 'good credit' card holders. Notice that I said holder, NOT user. If they don't waive the annual fee, close the account. A note to the wise; read the fine print when dealing with credit card accounts. Credit card companies will hurt you on their interest rates, annual fees, late fees, and special/teaser offers. Know that it has never been in your favor to pay just the <u>minimum</u> payment amount on your credit card bill. *But, I will show you a little later, the one exception where I would do this for a very short time. For those of you who must use a credit card, it is best to always pay off the charged amount in full before 30 days are up. In my opinion credit cards should never be used, unless it's a real emergency and there is no other way.

Would you believe that you can get to a debt-free, financially-free life where you can pay cash instead of charging it? Yes, believe it! You are on your way.

What I am going to show you can start working within a month - even within weeks for a lot of people. I am going to show you what I call **'the instant gratification way'**. This is debt payoff on steroids.

So here it is. The instant gratification way is to pay off 'first' the bills that have the <u>lowest</u> <u>total</u> <u>amount to pay off</u>. Stay with me now.

Don't quit already. I told you it is so simple that you might not believe me. Yes, you will start by paying off your lowest or smallest bill **first**. I hear you… "How can I pay off my lowest bills when I don't even have an extra fifty dollars left from my paycheck?", "Are you nuts, I am living from paycheck to paycheck now, how can I pay off any bills?", and "I can hardly make the monthly payments now, I don't have any paying off money." Don't worry, you and I will solve that problem.

This can be done. It can be done quickly. And **you can do it**. Have a little trust in this debt payoff plan, a little belief in yourself, <u>**add your best effort and actions**</u>, and it's all done - Debt freedom!

When you become debt free, and you will, and when you decide that you would like to have **financial freedom for life**, contact me and I will show you how. And yes, you can contact me even before you become debt-free. But, <u>you must have truly decided</u> that you really **want** it. *This also will help you find **more** extra money. It will be **financial freedom for life** on steroids – quick and in a hurry!

Let's get started. Stay with me now.

STEP ONE

Make a list of your bills

Write a list, names and total amounts, of all your bills: credit cards, car loans, doctor bills, furniture loans, house loan, etc. Do NOT write down any on-going monthly bills such as your utilities (electric, water, gas), apartment/house rent, cell/mobile bill – these are not total payoff bills, <u>unless</u> some of these are back-due bills that need to be paid off.

Now arrange the bills from low to high in order of the amounts to pay off. You can even arrange them from high to low as long as you understand that your **'first' target bill** to pay off is the bill with the lowest total amount of all the bills that need to be paid off. Next, number the bills starting with <u>the **lowest total amount bill** being #1</u>. Continue with numbering #2, #3, etc. to the last bill which is the highest amount bill. This is just to <u>keep you focused on the right bill to be paid off first, second, third, etc</u>. It is important to pay your bills off in order with the lowest total/balance due being first. Remember, this is instant gratification on steroids. Stay in order.

STEP TWO

Where to find the money to pay off your bills

Ok, now that you know which bills to pay off first, it's time to show you where to get the money to pay the bills off. We know what is said when someone assume something. I am going to take a chance and assume here. I am going to assume that you are making the full regular monthly payment on each of your bills. I hope that went over well?

Maybe it didn't? In that case, I am going to assume one last time. I am going to assume that you are making at least some kind of the regular monthly payment on each of your bills. I hope that went over even better?

My point is that the monthly regular payments that you are making now, regardless of how small or large, will be added to your new found extra monies in order for you to make larger payments. So keep that in mind.

To start your debt payoff with a big bang, you need to find extra money. I hear you again…"You nut, where am I going to find extra money?" and "Listen crazy, I live from paycheck to paycheck, what extra money?" Wait, don't quit yet. You are not a quitter. Remember, have a little trust in this debt payoff plan, have a little belief in yourself, give a little effort, and it can be done.

Now that you have a little trust and a little belief, this is where you give a little effort. Below is a list where you can find extra money. You can use one, a few, or all of the suggestions if you choose. Of course, the more suggestions you use that I listed below, the more money you will find. You will definitely find money.

Most of us waste so much weekly and monthly money after (and sometimes before) we pay the monthly bills. I think it's called discretionary spending money. This is money that we choose to spend how and when, on what and where. Now is the time for you to choose to make the effort to use this money to get out of the debt hole that you have discretionarily dug for yourself. A decision of commitment to get DEBT-FREE!

Where to find the extra monies:

1. Stop ordering in or picking up carryout (pizza, Chinese, McDonalds) for 1 to 4 weeks
2. Stop going out to dinner for 1 to 4 weeks
3. Stop going out to the movie theater for 1 to 4 weeks
4. Stop shopping for clothes, shoes, etc. for 1 to 8 weeks (wear what's in your closet)
5. Cut off Cable TV for 3 to 6 months [breathe, you will live]
6. Drop all the Cable TV premier channels (HBO, Showtime), and keep just basic Cable TV for 3 to 6 months [breathe, you will live]
7. Limit getting Blockbusters DVD movies to just 1 a month for 3 to 6 months
8. Stop out-of-town trips for 3 to 6 months
9. Take brown-bag-it lunch to work for 1 to 8 weeks
10. Don't vacation out of state this year (your county or state has a lot of sights to see)
11. Start getting your hair and nails done only once a month [breathe, you will live]
12. Stop going to happy-hour sport bars and clubs for 1 to 3 months
13. Carpool to work for 1 to 3 months
14. Cut back the snacks (ice cream, cookies, candy, chips, sodas) when grocery shopping
15. Get a temporary part-time job for 1 or 2 days a week for 1 to 2 months
16. Cut down on your Christmas shopping (gifts, toys) this year

17. Set your A/C higher and your Heat lower to bring down monthly utility bills

18. Stop buying bottled water, start using a filter on your faucet (it's cheaper)

19. Cancel magazine and newspaper subscriptions for 3 to 6 months (some of these can be read at the public library)

20. Shop around to lower your auto, homeowners, or renters insurance (to get a free, no obligation quote call 1-877-855-8111 and give the code: E6265 ALSTON)

21. Cut back on your cell phone minutes [breathe, you will live]

22. Cut back on beer, wine, liquor (buy less/drink less) [breathe, you will live]

23. Cook inexpensive meals and freeze leftovers for another meal time

24. Cut back on smoking cigarettes, cigars, pipes [breathe, you will live]

25. Cut back on drinking regular or espresso coffee [breathe, you will live]

26. Request a temporary 3-6 months waiver on your student loan payment

27. Sell an item of value that you own (used car, a desk, etc)

You get the idea. Find the extra money to get started from wherever you can …without borrowing it. You do NOT need to borrow from anyone, anywhere, any way! Once again, do NOT borrow any money to start your debt payoff plan. If you borrow the extra money this payoff plan will probably NOT work for you. Borrowing money defeats your goal of paying off your debt. You will be adding to your debt and taking yourself deeper into the hole. Enough said about borrowing.

Those twenty-seven suggestions I gave should get you started on finding quite a bit of extra money. I'm guessing that if you gave a little thought and effort you could come up with another twenty-seven or more ways to find more extra money. Just to stay ahead of the twenty-seven that you might come up with on your own, let me give you one more suggestion.

This is the competitiveness in me: that extra effort of pushing, doing, and giving just a little bit more.

28. This is a quick temporary way to find extra money. If you already have bad credit, you can take the monthly payment money from some of the other bills temporary for 1 or 2 months just to get started. The other bills (say #3 and #4, and maybe #5) that you will be taking their monthly payment money from, will get paid off sooner than you and the bill collectors ever thought possible any way. By the second or third month that you decide to start back the monthly payment on #3 and #4, you will be making a bigger payment on them or a possible full and final pay-off payment on one or both. Yes, the bill collectors for #3 and #4 will call you when you don't make the payment. So what? If they were calling in the first place, they will just continue to call. If they were not calling you before, then just welcome them to the club and tell them that the bill will be paid off in 2 to 3 months. You already have bad credit, what are they going to do? Whether a few of your creditors or all of your creditors marked you with bad credit, you have bad credit! It won't be bad credit for long [Breathe, you will live].

Important:

There are debts which you must keep paying until totally paid. Do NOT temporary stop these, (A) Federal and State taxes because your paycheck could be garnished, and above all keep paying your (B) CHILD SUPPORT because your child/children needs it first and foremost, and your paycheck could be garnished or you could go straight to jail.

If you got into this debt hole while making the same money you now make, then it should be enough money to get you out of the hole now. Most of us make enough money now, to get out of the debt we're in now.

For some of you that have been downsized and are now working a lower paying job, you can still do this. It will just be a little slower and take a little longer. Don't quit. Remember, have a little trust in this debt payoff plan, a little belief in yourself, give a little more effort, and it will be done – debt freedom! Yes, you can still do this. You have nothing to lose but debt, stress, and worry. Your gain will be good credit, and more money to save, invest, and spend. Stay with me now. Don't quit.

Have you ever heard the slogan 'no pain, no gain'? Here's a slogan for us, 'little effort of pain, equals a big gain'. For those of you that will give the little effort to find the extra money, I say well done because you will be debt free.

Sad to say, but some of you will make the 'little effort' worst than it really is. Remember our mindset of instant gratification? There are some who will take 'now' too far. They want it now, not weeks or months from now, but right now even though they have not put forth any effort to receive it now.

Let me stop here and tell you about someone that received the early version of this Debt Payoff Plan. It worked then, and now it has been updated to work even better. I will not use the words he, she, him, or her so as not to point to a man or woman. I will let you guess which one (smile). This person (I knew them personally) complained about some of the suggestions that were in the plan (12 at that time). If I had been standing face to face with them when I suggested they use #5 and #6 above, I believed they would have

knocked me down. They got mad as h_ _ _. They really fussed me out. They finally said that they would "try" a few of the suggestions because they didn't have any of their own at the time.

I didn't hear from them again, until three months ago (almost four years) I ran into this person, and the first thing they wanted to know if they could purchase the Debt Payoff Plan. I said to them that "once you have followed the steps and gotten out of debt, I would think that you would stay out of debt or at least remember how to get out of debt again, if necessary". They admitted that they never followed the plan because they were so upset about cutting off the Cable TV (their main entertainment) that they laid it down, forgot about it, and lost it. They also admitted that their debt (new bills with some of the same old bills) were worst than four years ago.

They did purchase the Debt Payoff Plan again. Will they follow the plan this time to get debt free? Who knows? How did they stand the stress and worry for almost four more years? Was that 'no pain, no gain'? Or was that 'a lot of pain, no gain?

If you noticed, I keep saying that if you follow this debt payoff plan you will have "more money to save, invest, and spend". You will, when you are debt free. But, for right now while you are following (doing) this plan you should stop putting money into your savings account. I hear you once again… "Are you crazy, what savings account?" and "Listen nut, I have no money to save." Believe it or not, there are those that have learned the lesson that come h_ _ _ or high water, they pay themselves first regardless of the debt. Some of us have not yet learned. When you are out of debt you will start paying yourself first, too. But, that's down the road a bit.

Now, why would I say stop depositing money into your saving account? Most people savings account is nothing more than their emergency funds account for when an emergency arise or a vacation account. I say stop because as you pay off bills, you will have that bill's regular monthly payment plus all of the weekly and monthly extra money that you have found, where as you can use for an emergency if needed.

Wow! Stop the press. Was that suggestion number 29 or what? It's that extra effort, again.

28. Stop depositing money into your savings account. Take this regular money deposit and add it to your 'snowball' payoff money for a quick start. New found money! You can start back saving even more money when your bills are gone, gone, gone.

The name I have given to all of this weekly and monthly extra found money and the monthly regular payment money is 'SNOWBALL payoff money'. Snowball because this payoff money will just keep growing and growing, larger and larger, bigger and bigger into hundreds of dollars a month as you pay off each bill and as you find other extra money. Just like a snowball rolling down a hill – it's growing. For some of you your 'snowball' payoff money will grow bigger faster every week because you get paid weekly, while others get paid bi-weekly.

Here is how it will work. When a REAL (not fake) emergency comes up, you will just take the money from your 'snowball payoff money', and take care of the REAL emergency. The money that you did not have to take from the 'snowball payoff money' will still be paid on the target bill. If by chance, you had to use all of the 'snowball payoff money' to take care of the REAL emergency, do it. Now that the REAL

Emergency has been taken care of; you will go back to your regular debt payoff schedule and continue paying off bills from low to high starting back with the target bill that you should have made a payment on before the REAL emergency.

A REAL emergency should be the only reason to take any of the money from your growing 'snowball payoff money'. This REAL emergency should be your REAL emergency, NOT some emergency someone else made up just to use your money. People we know will do that to us.

Important:

Under no circumstances am I talking about stopping your retirement account. Your retirement is not an in-the-local-bank saving account. DO NOT stop your retirement account. PLEASE CONTINUE PUTTING MONEY INTO YOUR RETIREMENT ACCOUNT.

STEP THREE

The process of paying off your bills

Start by making your very first 'snowball' payment on your #1 bill, which is your lowest balance due bill. I have faith that for a lot of you, that payment will pay off your #1 bill completely. For some of you it will not. Remember, how big your 'snowball' depends on how big an effort you really put forth in finding as much extra money as you can.

If the first lowest bill was not paid off with that first payment, then you would make your second 'snowball' payment on that same #1 bill until it is paid off completely. You will not start to pay on your #2 bill until your #1 bill is totally paid off. If that first payment completely paid off your #1 bill, and you still have 'snowball' money left over, you will begin paying on #2 bill with that left-over 'snowball' money.

Remember; do NOT take any of the money out of the 'snowball' payoff money - unless it is for a REAL emergency for you. Do NOT waste it. Stay focused. Pay it on the next bill. If you continue to stay focused and stay on track, in three to six to twelve months you will be able to go back spending money on all the discretionary things that you used to spend money on. I hope that you would not want to go back to the majority of them.

Once #1 bill is all paid off, you will then permanently add #1 bill regular monthly

Payment to your 'snowball' payment, which will be added to #2 bill regular monthly payment, to be paid on #2 bill. When you have totally paid off your #2 bill, then you will move up to #3, etc. You will do this (paying off each bill) while still making your regular minimum monthly payments on your others bills. *This is my one exception to paying minimum monthly payments – for a short time.

Every time a bill is paid off you will permanently add the paid off bill regular monthly payment to your 'snowball' payment. Your 'snowball' payment will grow bigger and bigger. The bill payoffs will happen fast. Now don't quit just because you have gained a little breathing room. You are on track to win the race to Debt Freedom. Keep going until all your bills are completely paid off.

Now just imagine all the extra money that you will have to save, invest, and spend; and don't forget the good credit. You can even pay off your car and home years sooner, if you have a desire to.

Important:

You should try to talk to your Creditors to negotiate a lower total payoff amount on each bill. Negotiate a little early for bills #1, #2, and #3 before you start making the payoff payments. Then do the same a little early for all your other bills just before you start making the payoff payments. You will keep yourself from paying out a lot of money. Some if not all of your Creditors will negotiate with you due of our weak economy, and they want to get paid sooner (2-6 months) rather than later (next year) or maybe even never.

At the beginning I told you that this was a very simple debt payoff plan. Now it is time for you to see that it will work and work fast. It's time for you to take action, put forth the effort. Don't let your doubt, fear, and disbelief get in your way. Start it now! You have nothing to lose but debt, stress, and worry. Your gain will be good credit, and more money to save, invest, and spend.

I would love to hear from you. Please send me a short note to let me know just how well it has worked for you. I also want to thank you for trusting in me enough to purchase my DEBT PAYOFF PLAN manual.

As I said earlier, you can contact me about financial freedom for life anytime in your process of getting out of debt – beginning, during, or ending of debt. But, you must have made a decision to change your financial life for the better. That means stepping out of your comfort zone, taking action, staying focus, and being committed to your success. I will be glad to show you how. It will change your life - quick and in a hurry!

May **GOD** shower you with peace, prosperity, and happiness.

Thank you.

Melford Alston

PO Box 7059

Largo, MD 20792

SOMETHING TO THINK ABOUT

By Melford Alston

I want you to have more …. you deserve it.

Want more? That's a real simple question. Kind of like a no-brainer. Almost to the point of being, a real stupid question. Of course, you want more. All of us want more of something – love, money, clothes, time, respect, travel, peace, space, cars, friends, life, happiness, freedom, and more. We can have more. Yes, you and I, all of us can have more. We can have more of the things we want.

But, how bad do you want it? How bad do you want it? Most people never want it bad enough. That's sad. Even though, they are the ones that need it the most. Most people are working and living miserably comfortable. It's their comfort zone, but they are miserable.

Most people live their life as if they have another life just sitting there on the sideline waiting for them to live it after they have finished wasting their first life. Wake up! You have only one earthly life to live. So live it. Go for it. Control your thoughts; take action against your fears, change your attitude to "I can and I will" and live the lifestyle that you really want.

Some people get to moving and go after what they want because of their dreams. And some get to moving and go after what they want because of their fears. And then, there are those that get to moving and go after what they want because of their dreams and their fears – they are the ones that are really in a hurry. What moves you the most, your dreams of success or your fears of failure? If you can't get hooked onto your dreams of success, then get hooked onto your fears of staying exactly where you are right now … forever. That should get you moving forward out of your miserable comfort zone. So, get uncomfortable and succeed at making your life and your family's life a lot better.

I thought that I was in the group that moved forward just because of my dreams. As I got to moving forward I realized just how far back and down I was from my dreams. I knew then, that I was in that group that moved forward because of my dreams and my fears. I guest I was in a hurry.

'Something to think about' is not to make you feel down and out. This is a 'hello' wake up call. This is to pump you up, lift you up, and push you up. To stop you from walking around in a daze thinking thoughts that others want you to think. To get you to take the blindfold off your eyes and see that you are living a miserable comfortable existence. This is to get you to dream again. It's time for you to start turning your dreams into your wants, and your wants into your goals. This is to get you to start planning and taking action moving towards your wants and goals.

I am hoping that I can say something here that will slap you in the face, hit you across the head, shock your noodle, stomp your toe, hit you in the gut, and wake you up.

Want more? How bad do you want it? YOU WANT IT REAL BAD! Now, change your mindset. Go pursue it. Go build it. Go get it. It belongs to you. You deserve it. Expect to have it. Make it yours. It will be yours!

Here's something to think about …

***

Believe in GOD, have faith in his power, and thank him everyday.

***

Change your mindset. Change your vision.

Think differently. Think about the possibilities.

Think "what more can I do".

***

Push your expectations, expect more of yourself.

Push your possibilities. Stretch your efforts.

***

Write down, with deadline dates, your short and long term goals.

Write down your plan in steps to accomplish your goals.

Take action following your plan to reach your goals.

Expect to accomplish your goals.

***

Expand your vision.

Want to be number 1.

Expect to win.

***

Take complete control over your options and your decisions.

***

Know that you can do what you want to do, if you want to do it bad enough.

Start now, step forward, pursue, seek, push, do it now.

Follow your dreams.

***

It's best that you take great interest in your future.

Because that's where you'll be.

***

Stretch your mind.

Think what if.

Think why not.

***

Go do something different. Do it another way.

Teach yourself to ignore limits.

***

Mess up, screw up, fall down, but get up. Make it work.

Get your back from against the wall, step forward, step up, and make some changes.

Everything is over-come-able, if you want to over come it.

***

With challenges comes an inner strength to succeed. Believe it!

Your thoughts are powerful. You are the solution to your challenges.

***

You bring hope to others. Be a blessing to others, and others will be a blessing to you.

***

Things that want to grow keeps moving. Change your mindset. Change your habits.

The longer it takes you to change, the longer it takes you to grow.

***

You must dream. Dreams are your future reality.

Never let anyone or anything steal your dreams.

Build your reality on your dreams and your wants.

***

Talk to yourself. Let your mind know that your future is whatever you want it to be.

Put your mind in control of your body. Take action and keep it moving.

***

You failed today. So what? That's just one way not to do it.

Do it another way tomorrow. If you fail again. So what?

Do it another way the next day. You are not a failure.

You just discovered ways that it doesn't work. You are not a quitter.

You will do it until you win. And you will win!

***

Action overcomes, subdues, and conquers fear.

Take action now! Success is not an accident.

***

This is your moment, your hour, your day, your year.

Take it and know that this is your time.

***

Be competitive. Take the challenge. Take some risks.

Most people don't know just how successful they could be.

***

Surround yourself with positive people that are doing something about their lives.

Stay in a positive environment and you will become part of that positive environment.

***

Never be satisfied with being good at what you do … when great is out there.

***

Stop being a couch potato. Get off the sofa. Take your eyes and mind out of TV.

Do something different. Reprogram your thoughts. Read books and listen to tapes.

They will help you get to where you want to be.

***

Concentrate on your dreams and your goals.

Be willing to get uncomfortable. Get out of your comfort zone.

Make a decision to start on a goal today, and accomplish it tomorrow.

It will build your confidence. You will feel better about yourself.

***

Leave your past in the past. It will do you no good in your future.

You have gotten pass it. Now, step up and look forward to your future.

***

Have a bold vision. See the top in your mind's eye.

Move, run, drive for the top … the view is always better at the top.

At the top is where you want to be. See yourself at the top.

***

Stop living a life of existence. Design and build a lifestyle of quality for yourself.

Your dreams and goals are big. The world is big. How big a piece do you want?

***

Whether you are ready for it or not, the future is coming …. Everyday!

Be ready for it. Make some changes and make your future great.

***

Everyday is a new beginning. It is the first day of the rest of your life. Begin again.

***

Happiness is a choice. It's your choice. Make a decision to be happy.

***

Have compassion and respect for others. Be passionate about helping others.

***

Want success? Then go get it. It is up to you. You must be the one to do what it takes.

You must hold yourself accountable before you hold someone else accountable.

***

Are you sick and tired of being sick and tired of being sick and tired of being ....?

You want to change it. You can. You have a can-do attitude. Your want is powerful.

Think progress. Make a decision. Set priorities. Stay focus. Be aggressive.

Be determined. Think accomplishment. Expect to succeed. Succeed!

***

Never let today dictate your tomorrows. Think prosperity. Get inspired. Go get more.

***

Be on a quest for opportunity. Find something enterprising to be passionate about.

While working for someone else's gain (job), work for your gain (your own business).

Find a business system, believe in it, and follow it.

Work it part-time, grow and expand your business to full-time.

Copy what successful business people do. Model their work ethics.

Dream big, Set a goal, make a plan, take action, stay focused, and succeed.

***

Be flexible and adjust, work smart, take some risk, embrace change.

Change the things that have kept you broke.

Start paying yourself first.

***

Dream, but don't just be a dreamer. You must be a doer, an achiever of your dreams.

***

A can-do attitude is the difference.

Doers are willing to put forth the effort.

They are willing to pay the price for their success.

***

Take your future and your security into your own hands.

Think out of the 'job' box. Awake the entrepreneur in you.

Build your own destiny by becoming a business owner.

Use your Just Over Broke, as a stepping stone into your own business.

***

Stop worrying about how things will turn out.

Be confidence that you can overcome all challenges.

Have faith that GOD will work wonders in your life.

***

Commit to do something you said you would do. Set a goal. Be dedicated.

Work smart to accomplish it. Stay focus. Be determined. Never quit.

***

Think big. Think wide. Think deep. Now add some action to it.

What you put into it is what you get out of it. It's out there … waiting.

***

You should want something better. Want to be financially free.

You should focus on financial security rather than job security.

Find a business opportunity to secure your financial future.

Business ownership has power.

***

Where you are right now is just part of your journey.

***

There comes a time in your life, when finally you have had enough of ….

too little, not much, nothing! You want more and you deserve to have it.

***

You need a Plan B, when you have the same 168 hours a week (24 hrs x 7 days) that everyone else has, and you don't have time to …. ?!

***

Give yourself peace of mind. Take control of your time.

Have a desire to make a difference in your life.

Your can-do attitude will take you to greatness.

Design the life of your dreams.

***

Life will give you what you fight for. Know what you are fighting for.

Know who you are. Know that you are somebody important!

Get up and go fight for the lifestyle that you want to live.

***

Develop a sense of urgency. Talk to yourself. Feed your mind positive thoughts.

***

Be so very thankful for what you now have, as you ask GOD for the more that you want. Do your part with a good heart. GOD will give it to you in abundance.

***

Never worry about people laughing at you. Challenges make you stronger.

***

Stay focus on your dreams and you will accomplish your goals.

***

Never let anyone rent space in your head.

***

Make a decision to walk the narrow path to success. Yes, you can succeed.

Get pass the no when someone tells you no, keep yes in your mindset.

Yes, you can do more than you thought you could. Yes, you will win.

Fight for financial freedom. Have a plan B. Create your own destiny.

***

USA is still the land of opportunity. Find your piece of the opportunity pie.

It's not… do you want a piece? It's… how BIG a piece do you want!

You and your family deserve a big piece. Don't just live. Live a lifestyle.

***

If you keep on doing the same old things the same old way, you will get the same old things the same old way. It's called 'Not having a clue'.

If you keep on doing the same old things the same old way, and expecting something different. It's called 'Ludicrous'.

Don't accept the misery. Change the way you do it. Or do something else.

***

Stop making excuses, stop blaming others. Accept the truth. Accept responsibility.

It doesn't have to be this way. Stand up, change your mindset, and change your life.

***

Riding the fence is half-of-a-life. Refuse to live in fear. Refuse to accept unhappiness.

Make a decision. Make a commitment to make a change. You deserve joy everyday.

***

You can do anything you want to. Want to. Want more.

***

Your belief, your attitude, your commitment, and your actions will get you your dreams.

***

Winning is a mindset – set your mind on thoughts of winning.

Thoughts are real. Control your mind. Thoughts can become your reality.

***

It's OK to be different. Be beyond what is usual – be extraordinary!

***

Your results today were your yesterday's decisions and actions.

Your decisions and actions today will be your tomorrow's results.

We have choices. Decide wisely, take massive action, get big results.

***

Your earning potential is what you think it is, whether it's $30,000 or $300,000.

Whatever amount you keep thinking about, you CAN make it so.

***

Change: to be different or make different, to alter, adjust, shift, remodel, transfer,

replace, transform, it is an act or result.

The ability to adapt is the ability to change.

Change is what it is – change! It is what you need. Fear not.

***

Decide what you want. Now decide what you are willing to exchange for it.

Show up. Put forth the work. Be willing to pay the price everyday.

***

What matters most is how you see yourself.

Don't like what you see? Change it. You have the power to change.

***

In fighting the enemy, sometimes you have to fight the "in of me" within.

Stop doubting yourself. Have courage. Your actions will conquer your fears.

Fear not, GOD is with you always. Ask him for guidance. Pray to him.

***

Financial freedom is not free. There is a price to pay. That price is your effort and time.

Get off the couch, cut off the TV, and go find a way to get financially free.

***

Your life revolves around a job.

You have NO control of your time or your money. The job do.

Your own business can revolve around your life.

You would have control over your time and your money.

Find a business system that you can be passionate about. Become a business owner.

***

Debt will keep you in bondage.

The rich ruleth over the poor, and the

borrower is servant to the lender. – Proverbs 22:7

***

A positive environment is very important. Stay away from negativity.

Surround yourself with people that are doing something about their wants, their goals.

***

"Your job" is not your job. It doesn't belong to you. That job belongs to your employer.

You have no ownership of that job. Your employer has power.

Find something you can have ownership of. Business ownership has power.

***

Your words and your actions have to be on the same track running at the same speed,

to accomplish what you said you would do. Go get it done.

***

If you don't make a change, won't the next 5 years be the same as the last 5 years?

***

The power of your thoughts has no limitations.

Your thought pattern will attract things to you.

Make it a habit to think powerful thoughts of good.

Master your thoughts and control your destiny.

***

For GOD hath not given us the spirit of fear;

but of power, and of love, and of a sound mind. – Timothy 1:7

*****

Every statement that read 'you' and 'your', replace them with 'I', 'my', or 'me'. Read them again. Make the statements yours. Read them with ownership. Place them into your heart and mind. Believe them as you say them out loud. Thoughts are so very powerful. Thoughts are things. They will change your mindset; your life.

****

This is year 2010, have you heard that there have been over 8 million JOBS lost during this recession? It's true. Everyday it's in the news about companies cutting JOBS or outsourcing JOBS to other countries. Question: Would you still buy from a company that you know is outsourcing JOBS to other countries? There are massive EMPLOYEE layoffs, downsized EMPLOYEES, fired EMPLOYEES, furloughed EMPLOYEES, and "good government JOB" EMPLOYEES that have been cut. And it looks as if there will be more.

Did you notice that the word JOBS are related to the word EMPLOYEES? There might not be anything wrong with being an employee on a job – for awhile. But, the job should

be used as a stepping stone to something much better. My point is, you need something that an employer can NOT take away from you.

You should own your own business! Work the days you want to work. Give yourself a raise when you want to. Work to build the lifestyle that you want. Opportunities to own your own business are all around you. You can even keep the job that you now have (if it hasn't been taken away already) while you build your business part time. There are a lot of businesses that you can work from home.

Haven't you dreamed of being your own boss, choosing your own work hours and your compensation? If you haven't, then now is the time to dream about it, think on it, plan it, and do it. Tough times call for tough decisions. Don't wait for times to get worst for you. You don't have to quit your job now, but it's best to start your part time business now. You can do this without jeopardizing your present job. But, understand that there is no such thing as a "job for life". Don't wait until you hear or see the word 'downsized' next to your name. Look for an entrepreneurial opportunity that you can be passionate about. Build something now that will belong to you and your family.

Questions: Do you have an open mind? How many sources of income do you have? How many times a week would you like to get paid? Would you like to do something different in your life? Are you satisfied with your income? Would you like to take off without your boss's permission? Are you open to making extra money? Would you like to work from home part time or full time? Could you use a bigger paycheck? Do you enjoy getting paid for helping people?

Please don't use excuses to set yourself up to fail before you even start changing your life. Excuse: I don't have the time, I'm too busy. Is that busy building your employer's business? Don't you have the same 168 hours a week that everyone else have? If not now, when? Excuse: Money is not everything. That's right, but money runs a close second to the air you breathe when it comes to you paying your mortgage/rent, buying food, and putting gas in the car. Excuse: My family and I are living OK. What do OK mean? Is that good or great? Is that living the lifestyle that you want? Is the family really happy living the way they are? Excuse: My job is secure. Oh, you must own the company you work for? Ever seen an ostrich with its head in a hole? It doesn't cover its butt – it's really exposed. Ever heard "don't put all your eggs in one basket" or "you need a back-up plan"? So, why do we put all of 'our hope for a successful future and great retirement' into working that job everyday with no 'Plan B' whatsoever?

I am NOT trying to scare you. I am trying to inspire you to reach for some of the things that you want in life – for you and your family. I am NOT trying to put anyone down. I don't want you to end up years from now, thinking and saying "I should of, could of, did this and did that for myself and my family". Most of us have NOT put away, saved or invested, enough to retire on. Yet, some of us still think that we can live off of social security and what we have saved. Here's a thought; If 100% of your bring home pay is NOT enough now, then how is 40% of that bring home pay going to be enough later?

Want more, now and later.

Start right now by changing your mindset with positive thoughts. Have a can-do attitude. You can give your family and yourself a better quality of life. You are a winner. Expect to win and you will win.

Please use my 'Debt Payoff Plan', it will definitely help you. And I hope I have inspired and motivated you with 'Something To Think About'.

As I said earlier, when you decide that you would like to have financial freedom for life, contact me and I will gladly show you how.

Most important of all, remember that GOD is with you always. Talk to him.

Thank you, again.

Melford Alston

PO Box 7059

Largo, MD 20774

www.ingramcontent.com/pod-product-compliance
Lightning Source LLC
Chambersburg PA
CBHW070434180526
45158CB00017B/1249